The Body Positive Journal

The Body Positive Journal

Virgie Tovar

Illustrations by Lucila Perini

CHRONICLE BOOKS
SAN FRANCISCO

Text copyright © 2022 by Virgie Tovar.

All rights reserved. No part of this book may be reproduced in any form without written permission from the publisher.

ISBN 978-1-7972-1445-0

Manufactured in China.

MIX
Paper from responsible sources
FSC™ C008047

Illustrations by Lucila Perini.
Design by Lizzie Vaughan.

10 9 8 7 6 5 4 3 2

Chronicle books and gifts are available at special quantity discounts to corporations, professional associations, literacy programs, and other organizations. For details and discount information, please contact our premiums department at corporatesales@chroniclebooks.com or at 1-800-759-0190.

Chronicle Books LLC
680 Second Street
San Francisco, California 94107
www.chroniclebooks.com

Contents

Introduction

Let's Start Off with a Fact: Your Body Is Precious Beyond Imagination
9

Rage Pages
12

Brag Book
18

Part 1

There Is Absolutely Nothing Wrong with Your Body

The Incredibly True and Entirely Untold Story of Your Body
25

Part 2

Grow the Relationship You Want with Your Body

Plants Teach Us Everything We Need to Know About Having a Body
59

Part 3

Move and Eat for Fun

Bye-Bye, Body Goals. Hello, Unconditional Self-Worth!

87

Part 4

You Had a BBID (Bad Body Image Day)

Anger Is Fire

139

Part 5

Your Body Does Not Exist for Other People. It Exists for You. Protect It.

The High Art of Boundaries

171

Introduction

Let's Start Off with a Fact: Your Body Is Precious Beyond Imagination

This journal is about helping you believe that and helping you create the relationship you want with your body.

Journaling is the process of discovering your own power: the power to reflect, learn, problem-solve, emote; to be vulnerable, self-aware, and honest; to know that no matter how terrible yesterday was, there's always a blank slate that's waiting for you if you just turn the page. These are the building blocks of transformation—on any scale.

Creating the relationship you want with your body is actually pretty simple: Keep finding and doing more stuff that makes you feel good. Yup, that's actually kinda it.

Don't underestimate the power of the things that make humans feel good. We get the most pleasure from friendship, fairness, intimacy, unconditional acceptance, a sense of safety, care, and love. These experiences have the power to change the world, too. Almost everything we do as humans—no matter how misguided we might feel—is in pursuit of those things. When we trust ourselves and we trust the power of that pursuit of pleasure, we are unstoppable.

The key word here is "simple." This word underscores actions that you as a human being have an intrinsic ability to do. You're coming up against a lot of cultural noise that makes the simplest things really hard. Take eating, for example. Most of us can agree that the act of eating is pretty simple: Get food, put in mouth, chew, swallow, feel the yum. But we all know that this simple act has become this huge, terrifying thing. Guess what? It doesn't have to be. Keep it simple. You need that precious mental energy and brain juice for bigger and better things.

It can be hard to actually figure out which things make us feel embodied, seen, and nourished. If you're having a hard time, it may mean you don't have the tools or support you need to get the outcome you want. This journal is here to give you a little support, but mostly to show you how rad you already are, help you polish off some old tools you haven't used in a while, and build some new ones to your exact specifications. This journal is here to help you notice the stuff that's already in your life that makes you feel good, discover new good stuff, and help you keep going back to that feeling.

The tools that help us again and again as we pave the path to more good stuff are also pretty simple: Notice the feelings you're having, set boundaries, practice listening to your intuition, do more things for the sake of fun (not for goals), call out trash when you see it. Repeat. Throughout this journal there will be opportunities to practice, hone, contemplate, celebrate, and scheme.

As you work through this journal, let your mind start seeing the good stuff as the "simple" stuff, and seeing the stuff that the culture piles onto that simple stuff as "entirely not necessary, thank you very much." That little reframe will do you wonders.

Now, how do you use this journal? Simple. However you want. There is no wrong way to use this journal.

The most important question to ask yourself is: How do *I* want to use this journal? What would make *me* feel good?

Think of this journal as a buffet. Take what you want. Leave what you don't. Check in before you start writing. Some good questions to ask before you dive into something in this journal are: Do I feel like doing this today? Can I handle doing this part today? If the answer to either is no, skip it. Come back later. You'll notice that some days, you'll feel excited about some things and not others. Nothing wrong with that. This is your intuition talking. Listen to it.

Up front, there's a section called Rage Pages. Anger is the focus of part 4, but even before then, you are encouraged to use these Rage Pages whenever you just need to unleash and vent. Getting comfortable with anger is an integral part of self-acceptance. There's also a section called Brag Book. This is for you to celebrate the small or large triumphs you experience as you do the work in this journal and in your life. Brag early, brag often.

There are prompts that ask you to doodle or write, or to do something out in the world and take field notes.

Do one prompt a day for a month; spread them out throughout the year; or just pick up the journal when you feel like it—no commitments. This journal can be a friend available at any time of the night or day.

Whatever you decide, remember that your goals are simple: Have fun. Feel good.

xoxo,
Virgie

Rage Pages

These pages are for days when you're pissed as hell! Rage on, babe. Vent your heart out. No apologies or rationalizations are allowed. Feel free to fill up every line.

Rage On, Babe!

Brag Book

These pages are dedicated to your accomplishments, no matter how small. Did you do something that felt good? Put together a killer outfit? Self-advocate? Say no when you wanted to? Say yes when you meant it? Prioritize your comfort? Have an aha moment? Eat something yummy? The brag book wants all your brags—big and small. Brag early. Brag often.

Brag Often!

Part 1

There Is Absolutely Nothing Wrong with Your Body

The Incredibly True and Entirely Untold Story of Your Body

Deep in your cells is the knowledge of the very first living creature on the planet and the remembrance of when we were all stardust.

Deep in your chest, a heart beats.
Deep in your brain, ideas germinate.
Deep in your belly, wisdom grows.

Your feet work with your brain, legs, arms, and bones, and together they do untold calculus to move you from place to place. Your lungs perform complex chemistry, taking in oxygen and releasing carbon dioxide. Your eyes can detect thousands and thousands of colors. Your body—no matter how you feel about it—does this for you every single day.

Humans—all of us—are impossibly sophisticated and miraculous creatures, existing against the odds of every challenge we have faced throughout time. It's difficult to remember this when you believe your body is a problem that needs to be fixed.

Your body is not the problem.
The way you've been taught
to *see* your body is.

Imagine you are going through an art gallery, and your guide—instead of telling you how interesting and beautiful every painting is—spends their time complaining about how every painting needs more blue in it or criticizing the paintings that don't look enough like a Picasso. With a guide like that, you might forget you're surrounded by masterpieces.

The guide is our culture.
The masterpiece is you.
It's all of us.

Remember that you're art.
Remember that you're art.

But First, a Permission Slip to Exist Exactly As You Are

_____
YOUR FULL NAME

This permission slip entitles the signee to **EXIST FULLY**, *completely*, and TOTALLY IN THEIR HUMAN BODY without need for shame, apology, or any other restriction on their ability to *thrive*. Once signed, this permission slip shall remain in effect throughout the **UNIVERSE** from now UNTIL THE END OF TIME.

_____

YOUR SIGNATURE

_____

DATE

Yes, How You Feel Does Actually Matter

A lot of us think that a good life is one that looks impressive on paper or inspires envy in a photo: a particular kind of home, partner, family, car, wardrobe, and—yes—body. The reason people sacrifice so much to have that "picture-perfect" life is that we believe happiness moves from the outside in: If everything looks good on the outside, I'll feel good on the inside. *This is a fallacy.* This prompt is about redefining a good life from the inside out. Start inside—with how you feel. Move the question from, How do I want to look? to, How do I want to feel? So, how *do* you want to feel? How do you want to see and experience the world? What parts of your emotional self do you want to grow and develop? What makes you feel good?

This Journal Is Body Positive

What's Stopping You?

What's stopping you from having the relationship with your body that you want? Name the fears you have and obstacles you face in the following stop signs.

Remember

Fear doesn't have to stop you from doing things that are important to you. Fear is information about your past, not necessarily information about your future. Take your time to tend to that hurt part of you the same way you would support a scared pet or kid—without judgment and with massive compassion. Use your intuition to start with the least scary thing you've written down. Are there one or two actions you can take that will help you feel safe as you challenge yourself to face that scary thing? For example, make a date with yourself and put "Plan To Examine Life Changes While Sipping My Favorite Tea and Listening to Bossa Nova" on your calendar. Maybe you love tarot, and can ask the deck for some inspiration. Turn this emotionally challenging work into something special, something you look forward to. Repeat with the second least scary item. You'll gain tools along the way as you move up the fear chain! Write some ideas and plans below.

Notice the Small Stuff

Noticing how things and people make you feel is the first step to rebuilding intuition—that sacred, silent language your body speaks. Today, your job is to notice the things (like magazines, billboards, furniture, social media accounts, and environments) and people (like neighbors, family members, baristas, waiters, classmates, or colleagues) who make you feel good, safe, or comfortable in your body and the things and people who don't. Jot down realizations and details in your field notes.

Field Notes

This Is What Your Body Does

Write about your day, but instead of focusing on what happened (e.g., I drove to work ... I picked up lunch at ...), *focus on each cool thing your body did along the way today* (e.g., My eyes let me see ... My skin felt this sensation ... My fingers grasped ...).

You've Got This, Babe!

The New Normal

Research shows that the visual processing center in our brains can quickly recalibrate what body sizes and shapes we think of as "normal." Most of the bodies we see in the media are representative of about 1% of the human population. Today, it's time to find the other 99%! Find some positive images of people with diverse body sizes and shapes (social media is a great place to start). In your field notes, write about what it was like, how it made you feel, if you used certain hashtags to find images, and if anything surprised you.

Field Notes

Put Trash in the Trash

On each trash bin, write one body-shaming belief you're ready to throw away. Then imagine yourself shutting the lid of all these trash cans when you turn the page!

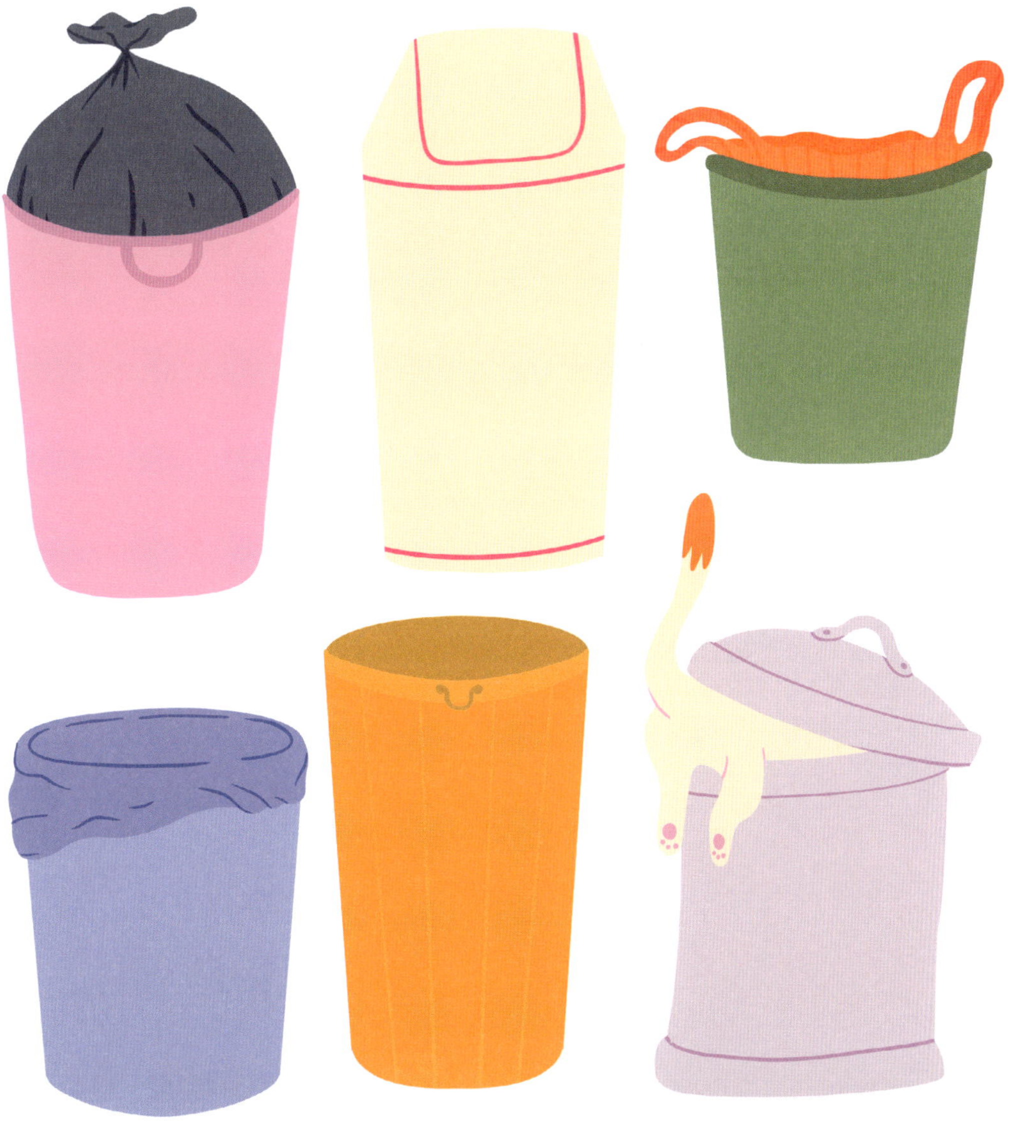

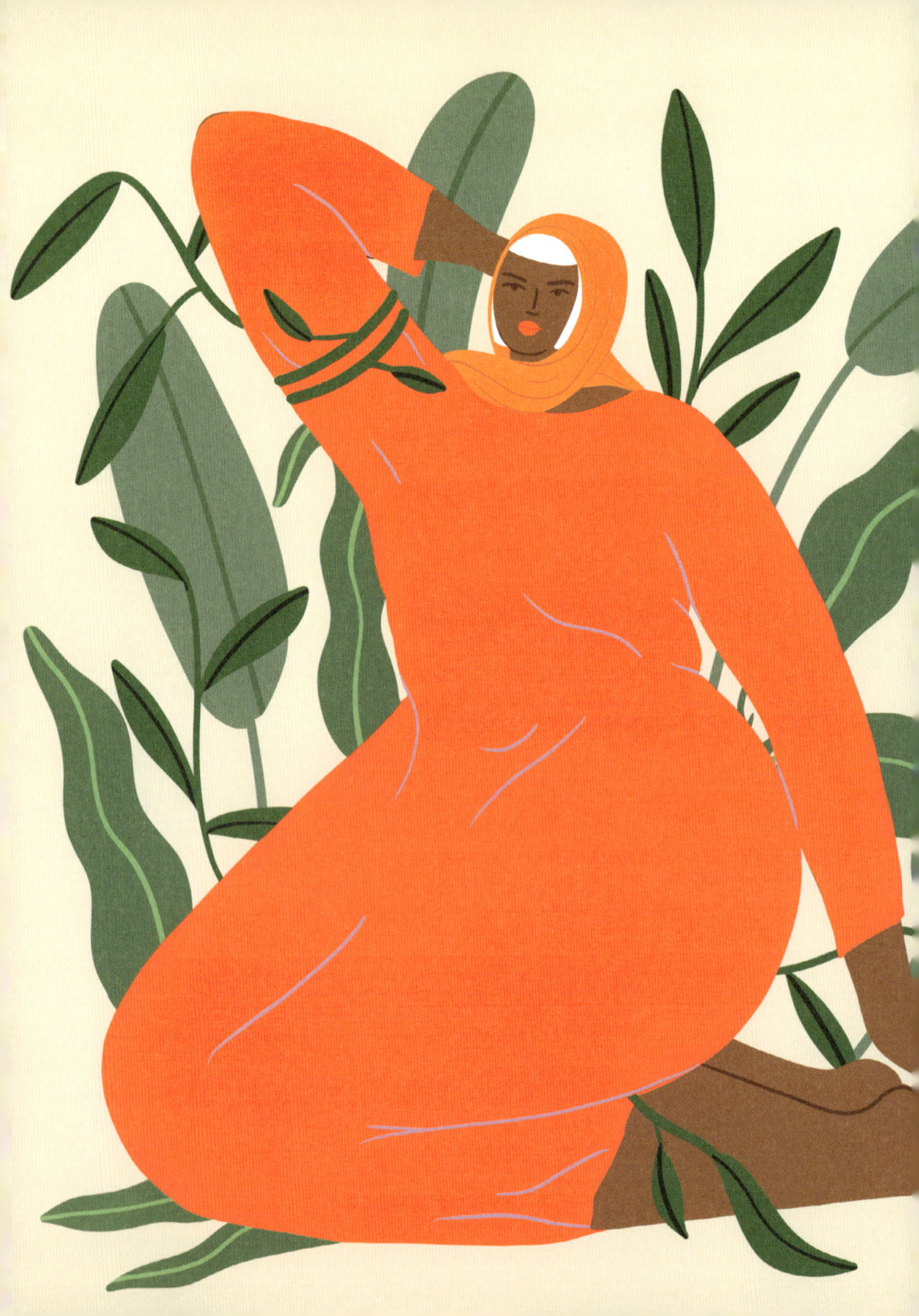

Part 2

Grow the Relationship You Want with Your Body

Plants Teach Us Everything We Need to Know About Having a Body

What if we saw people the way we see gardens? Our eyes light up when we see the prismatic combinations of leaves, flowers, trees, and grass. We would probably be pretty bummed if we walked into a garden that was filled with thousands of the exact same plant. And we would probably be pretty weirded out by a gardener who told us they were dedicated to making every species of plant look like the one they had decided was the best one. We don't look at a redwood tree and long for it to be a ficus. We don't look at a rose and ask why it doesn't look like a fern. We accept and love them each exactly the way they are. We know our lives are better with this multiplicity. We know the world couldn't exist without it.

Guess what? We can look at others—and ourselves—the same way!

Plants teach us a lot of important lessons about our bodies.

1. **Like plants, people come in all shapes and sizes, and we can recognize all of them as equally stunning and special.** Some people's bodies are like tall, wispy palms. Some are short and stocky succulents. Some bloom in wild, electric colors. Others are evergreens. Some have thorns. Others have big, unfurling leaves. We love seeing the differences in plants' shapes, colors, and textures, and we can apply that thinking to appreciate different bodies as well.

2. **It's OK that our bodies have different needs.** When we get a plant, we can usually find out how much light, water, and space it needs. Some plants need a lot of attention and others prefer to be left mostly alone. We don't see this diversity of needs as a deficit. We understand that each plant just has those needs. Like plants, we all need certain things to be OK, and different people have different needs. Your needs are unique and completely fine. You can nonjudgmentally accept these parts of yourself and your body.

3. **You don't need to have a different kind of body to be perfect.** Every year there are orchid expos across the globe. These events are bursting with tens of thousands of orchid enthusiasts who come from all over the world to see and buy orchids. Orchids require a lot of care; and yet so many people love them. On the flipside, many people don't. An orchid isn't going to change what it needs just because a person doesn't like orchids. A dandelion isn't going to try to become an orchid in hopes of making an orchid enthusiast happy. Like plants, you can just keep being yourself and trust that you are exactly right as you are. Like our cactus friends who are round and prickly, remember it is 100% awesome to be a chubster with an attitude. Like our attention-loving orchid pals, your needs are part of your unique magic. Body diversity—like plant diversity—includes not just the wispiest or the tallest, but also the roundest and the thorniest. The world needs all of it.

4. **It's OK to have unapologetic boundaries.** Plants have defense mechanisms—boundaries that keep them safe—such as sticky sap, sharp thorns,

or—like the Venus fly trap—enzymes that can turn insects into a nutritious soup. Cacti are very clear about their boundaries, which are *literally* pointy spines that protect their bodies. Similarly, people need boundaries to protect their physical bodies and feelings. Like a cactus's spines, boundaries help keep the nourishment we need inside ourselves when we're in harsh environments. And those boundaries can look different depending on what we each need as an individual.

5. **You are lovable even if all you do is hang out, sipping water in the sun all day.** There is so much pressure to be amazing and perfect and productive all the time! Take a lesson from plants: Their only job is to sit on a windowsill or a desk, drinking water and sunbathing. Yet they still fill up our hearts and bring us a smile. It's so easy to feel that we aren't worthy of this or that unless we work our butts off. Remember that even if you do absolutely nothing today (or for a week or a month or a year), it cannot change this fact: You are lovable, you are worthy, you are just right.

If I Were a Plant, I'd Be...

Describe yourself the way the proud owner of a plant nursery would. Using these pots as a guide, draw your very own unique plants.

What are your roots (the family, place, and experiences that have shaped who you've become)?

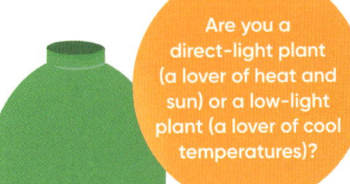

Are you a direct-light plant (a lover of heat and sun) or a low-light plant (a lover of cool temperatures)?

Do you have bright, small, large, or no flowers (is your style minimalist, maximalist, or somewhere in between)?

What else helps you thrive? Some plants seem to love when their human companions play them music; research suggests some plants really don't like to be touched. What about you?

Are you an indoor plant (who loves staying in) or an outdoor plant (who craves adventure)?

What's your species called? (Make it up!)

How often do you need to be watered (do you like lots of attention or to be left mostly alone)?

Do you need to live in a spacious pot (you love plenty of elbow room) or a small one (you prefer a cozy vibe)?

You Are Lovable Just Because You're You

You are worthy of love. That is a fact. What do you need to hear to feel convinced that you are worthy of love and care, no matter your size, shape, health status, or ability level? Write it down.

Instructions for Care

It would be ah-mazing if we could hand a little card detailing what we need and want to every new person we meet. This can be that card! Write out what you want to tell others about how you like to be cared for. What things make you feel appreciated, recognized, taken care of, and loved?

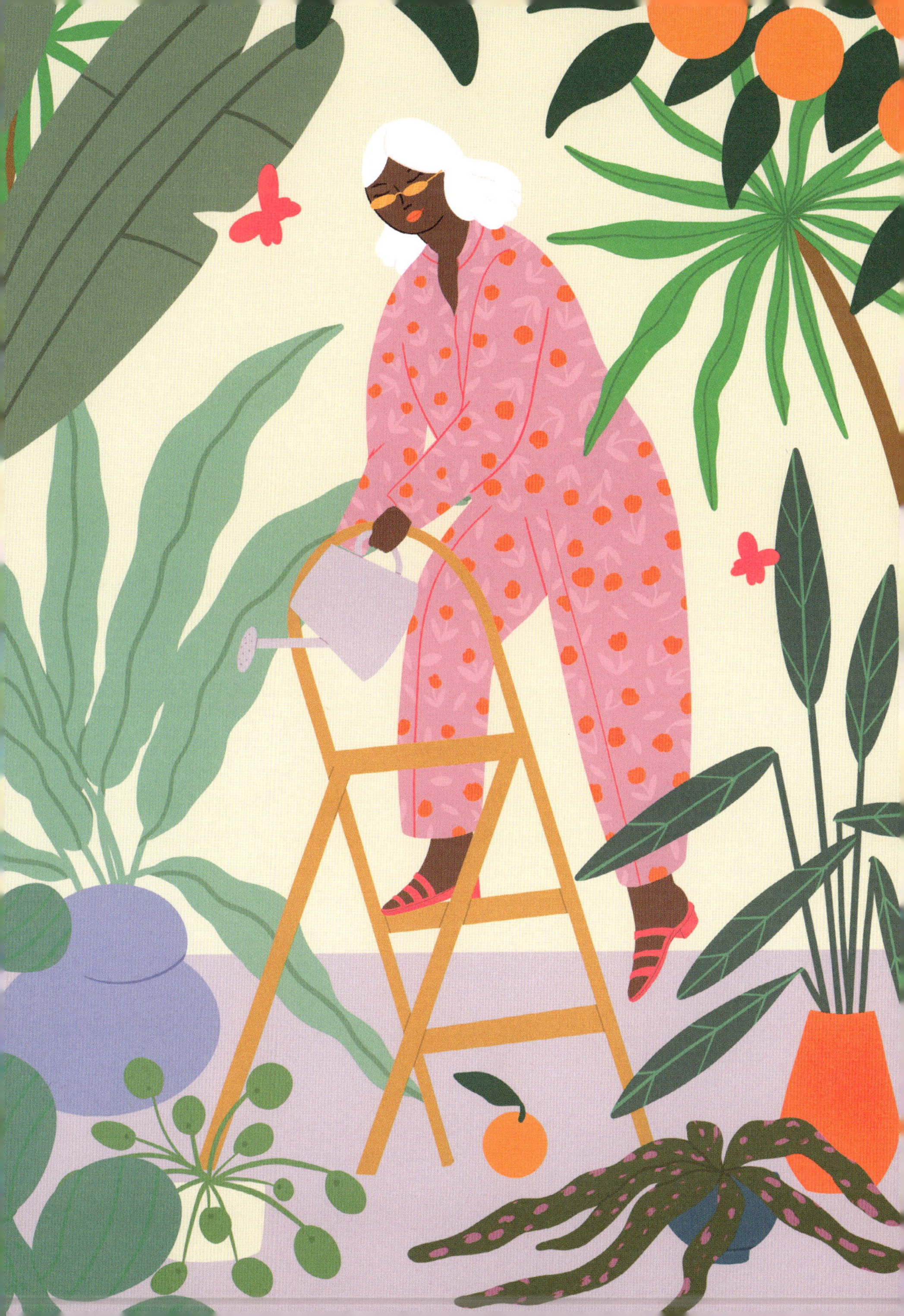

What Do You Need in Order to Grow?

On each of these flowers, write down a body-affirming idea or a practice that you'd like to do more of in order to help you grow.

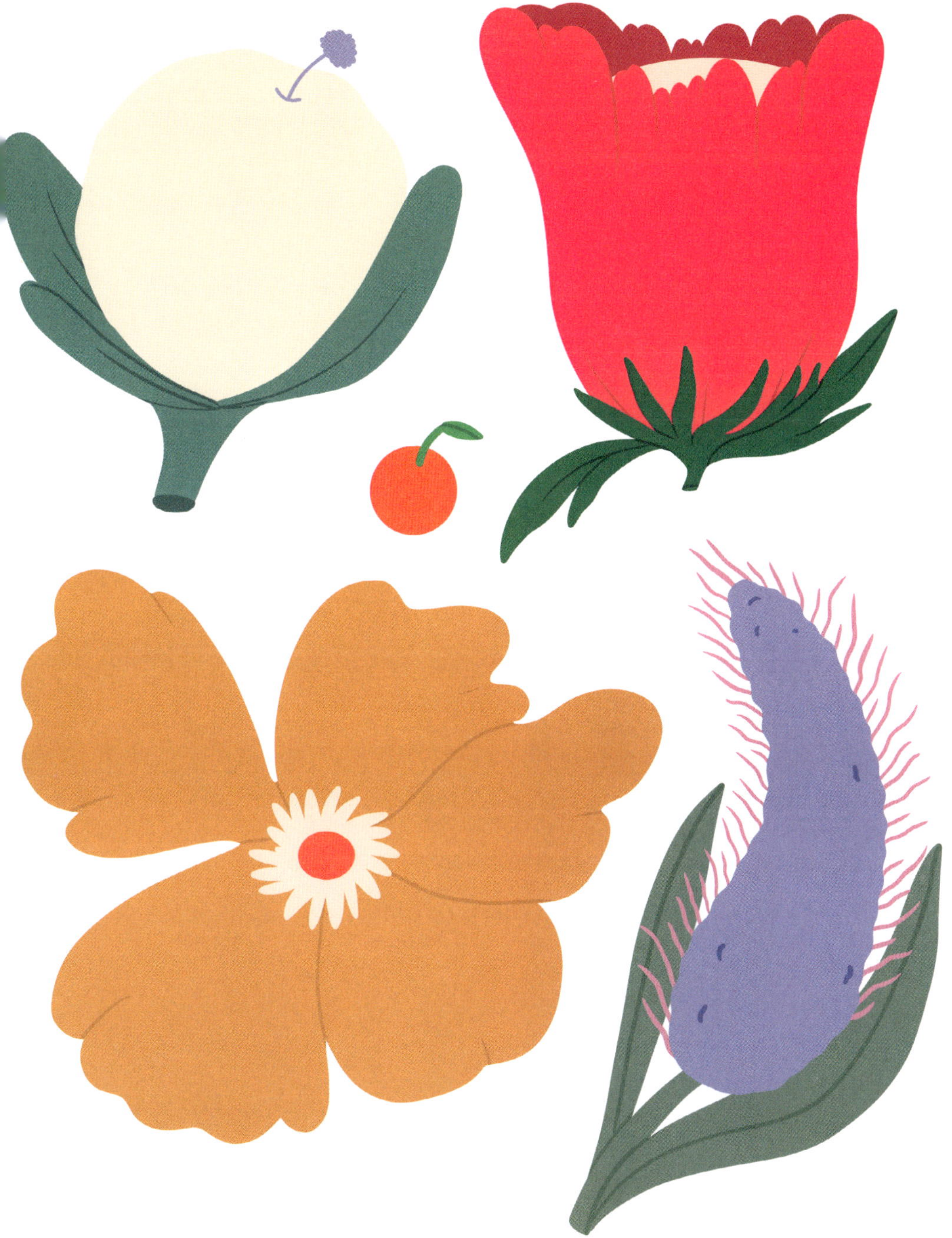

Channel Your Inner Cactus

A cactus's spines are a tangible physical boundary that lets other creatures know without a doubt if they've come too close and become a safety threat. Cacti have spines because they need to protect their internal sources of water and keep away anything that might diminish that life force. Similar to the cactus, you can provide yourself protection from many unwanted emotional and physical interactions if you unapologetically let your spines be known. Answering these questions can help you name the situations and behaviors that require you to channel your inner cactus.

→ What three words would you use to describe how it feels in your body when you don't like something?

1. _____

2. _____

3. _____

→ I don't like when other people do [blank] around me.

_____

_____

_____

_____

_____

_____

_____

_____

_____

→ How do you know when you're done with a situation or a person?

→ What does your body do when you feel like you're not being heard?

→ How does it feel in your body when you are angry?

→ What is one place or thing that makes you feel negative most of the time?

→ How do you know when you've hit a limit?

→ Someone will get pricked (receive my wrath) if they do [blank] to me.

Stop Hanging Out with People Who Steal Your Sunshine

Any plant parent will tell you that you've got to give your plants what they need and not let anything block their access to water and light. What if you protected yourself with the same ferocity? Write down the names of people who steal your precious resources. Next to their name, write down your plan for self-protection. Is it engaging with them less? Is it letting them know your Instructions for Care (page 72)? Is it taking extra time before you interact with them, allowing you to take some deep breaths and ground yourself? Get creative!

Sunshine Stealers   **My Self-Protection Plan**

Sunshine Stealers

My Self-Protection Plan

Sunshine Stealers	**My Self-Protection Plan**

Sunshine Stealers

My Self-Protection Plan

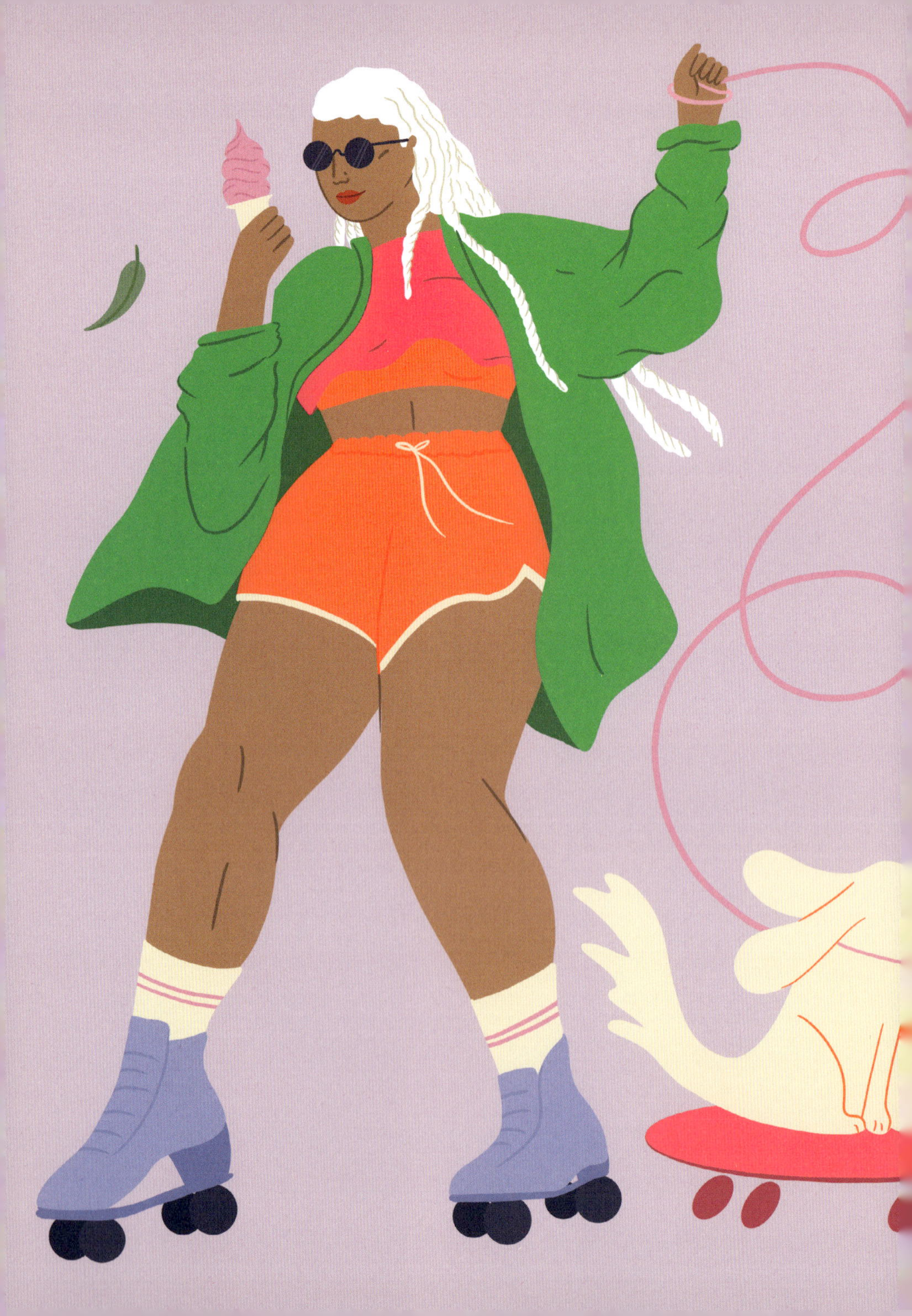

Part 3

Move and Eat for Fun

Bye-Bye, Body Goals.
Hello, Unconditional Self-Worth!

Part 3

Remember being a kid? You probably did all kinds of goofy, silly, weird, fun things with your body. You jumped on your bed (when no grown-ups were looking) or spent an hour trying to touch the highest branch of a tree. You dreamed of eating a sundae with thirty-two scoops of ice cream with whipped cream and sprinkles on top. You wiggled and jiggled. You ate Halloween candy like it was the last day on Earth. You rolled down hills. You ate with both hands and got food all over your face and didn't care. You danced when you heard a song you loved. You sweated. You ran. You laughed. You *did*. And there was no shame or sense of failure attached, because there was no goal other than having fun. So you couldn't do it wrong or miss your goal. All of these fun, silly kid things are perfectly legitimate examples of healthy moving and eating.

As we become adults, a lot of us learn that moving and eating are *primarily* things we do in order to control our body size or our health. There's always a goal: win a challenge, lose weight, "work off" our lunch, get our heart rates up, get praise from a coworker or someone who matters to us, just be "good."

What's the difference between "exercising" and "moving"? Exercise is just movement with a goal attached.

What's the difference between "diet" and "food"? Diet is just food with a goal attached.

For the record, having goals isn't a bad thing; but when you attach them to things like eating and moving—things we do every single day, all day long—you've got a recipe for some major anxiety.

When it comes to our bodies, a goal-oriented mindset really restricts the incredible range of motion our bodies are capable of. It also limits our body's natural capacity to work through hard feelings by stomping, singing, screaming, wiggling, jumping, and tapping our fingers and toes. Most importantly, it demolishes our body's natural capacity to feel joy fully.

When you attach moving and eating to your self-worth, you end up spending way too much time chasing an impossible goal. Why is it impossible?

Because how you eat and move have absolutely zero-zilch-nada-niente to do with your worth. Using food and movement to feel worthy is like trying to use pickles to buy a sports car. *Pickles just don't buy a sports car.* Nothing wrong with pickles—that's just not how they work.

Food doesn't have the power to make you good or bad. Movement doesn't have the power to make you worthy or unworthy.

You are always good.
You are always worthy.

You always, always deserve care, respect, and dignity—no matter how you eat or how you move your body. Got it?

Moving and eating can be spaces for lowering the stakes and growing self-worth: "I do this because I'm alive. I do this because I deserve to feel good. I do this because I'm worthy, unconditionally."

We can all learn a thing or two from our inner kid selves about how to have fun when we move, and definitely when we eat.

Always remember: You are still that kid. You will never lose that spirit. Sometimes adults forget that. But here's the good news: Fun is only ever as far as a rain puddle ready for hopping in or a plate of mashed potatoes waiting to be turned into a masterpiece.

Imagine It First

What could your life look like if you took the goals out of eating and moving and just tried doing them for fun? Would you experiment with adding stuff to the cream cheese (cinnamon? food coloring? rosemary? edible flowers?) for your morning bagel? Would you turn those old jeans into short shorts and throw a dance party for one? Go wild with your imagination!

This Journal Is Body Positive

You Deserve a Break (from Diet Culture) Today

We often don't realize how much pressure we feel to engage in judging our bodies and others'. Today, don't engage in talking about food (yours and others') or bodies (yours and others'). See how you feel. In your field notes, write about what it was like, how hard or easy it was, if there were awkward moments where you left someone hanging, and if you feel like it made your day more or less stressful.

Field Notes

You've Got This, Babe!

Lower the Stakes

We've been trained to fear that if we aren't constantly attempting to control the size of our bodies, bad things can and will happen to us. In other words, we're walking around *every* day feeling like *every* thing we put into or do with our bodies is very, very high-stakes. Think about it! Is there a tiny voice in your head constantly saying, "If I do this, I will be unlovable/become horribly ill/die/lose all control/ruin my entire day (or life)/become an evil troll octopus who eats children?" Creating a better relationship with your body means lowering the stakes—big time. This takes practice, but it starts with a change in script. Write down your most common "If I do (blank), then (blank) will happen" thoughts. Then rewrite them with a less catastrophic and more realistic ending.

Current Catastrophic Body Thought

If I _____ ,

then _____

_____ will happen.

Rewrite

If I _____ ,

then _____

_____ will happen.

Current Catastrophic Body Thought

If I _____ ,

then _____

_____ will happen.

Rewrite

If I _____ ,

then _____

_____ will happen.

Current Catastrophic Body Thought

If I _____ ,

then _____

_____ will happen.

Rewrite

If I _____ ,

then _____

_____ will happen.

Current Catastrophic Body Thought

If I _____ ,

then _____

_____ will happen.

Rewrite

If I _____ ,

then _____

_____ will happen.

Current Catastrophic Body Thought

If I _____ ,

then _____

_____ will happen.

Rewrite

If I _____ ,

then _____

_____ will happen.

Current Catastrophic Body Thought

If I _____ ,

then _____

_____ will happen.

Rewrite

If I _____ ,

then _____

_____ will happen.

Dear Food, I Love You

Write a love letter to your favorite food. Describe it adoringly. Focus on the details: smell, texture, flavor. Feel free to be extra.

This Journal Is Body Positive

Jiggle Like It's 1999

Jiggling is surprisingly powerful (and very, very fun). It's like turning your body into a human snow globe, shaking up energy and body parts. Put a timer on for one full minute. Spread out your arms and legs. Jiggle all your bits. Report back.

Comfort Is King

It's easier to be embodied—present in your physical body—when you feel comfortable. Comfort comes in two flavors: emotional and physical. They are interconnected. This section is about adding more comfort (both types!) to your daily life. Ready? Write down the things you interact with the most at home. Then rate them on a comfort scale of 1 through 10, with 1 being "really terrible" and 10 being "basically the best thing ever." After you're done, see the writing prompt following the score sheet.

Pieces of Furniture I Use the Most

Comfort score

1. _____

2. _____

3. _____

4. _____

5. _____

Items of Clothing I Wear the Most

		Comfort score
1.		
2.		
3.		
4.		
5.		

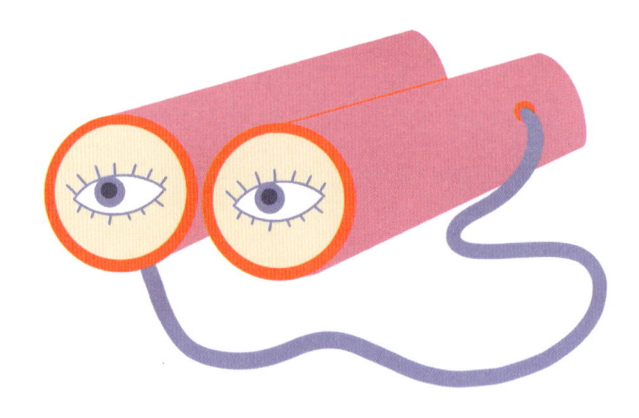

Places Where I Spend the Most Time

Comfort score

1. _____

2. _____

3. _____

4. _____

5. _____

→ The goal for this activity is to practice the skills of noticing, checking in with your body, and taking concrete steps to add more good stuff that your body likes into your life. So, take a look at the things on the list above that have a score of 6 or higher. How can you start spending more time with the high-comfort-score stuff? How might you phase out the low-comfort-score stuff? What steps can you take, moving forward, to make sure new things coming into your life are at a score of 6 or higher?

Double Chin for the Win

The days of taking the "flattering" selfie are officially over. Part of changing your relationship with your body means familiarizing yourself with all of your body as it currently exists, in all of its perfectly excellent angles. So today your task is to take a selfie that challenges you—a selfie that captures you just the way you are. Maybe take a selfie from below your jawline or while snacking. Capture a part of your body you have a hard time loving. You could also place the camera on the floor, set the timer, and relax your face completely. In your field notes, write honestly about how that felt. Then describe the photo using positive, affirming language.

Field Notes

You've Got This, Babe!

Don't Need Permish to Eat Things That Are Delish

Yes, you deserve to eat delicious things and enjoy them! For the duration of eating something delicious, you have been granted a moratorium on shame, guilt, or overthinking. Report back.

Field Notes

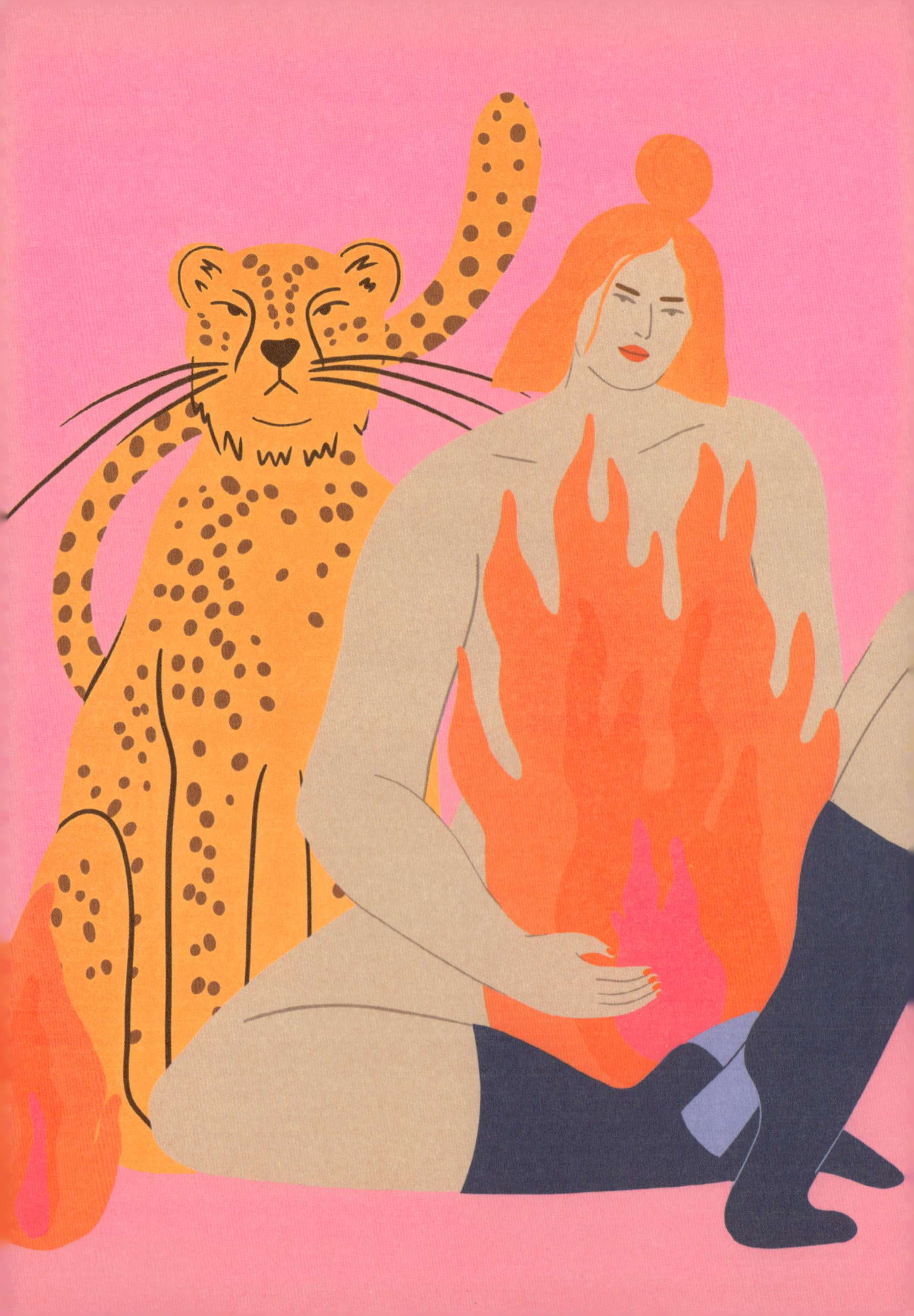

Part 4

You Had a BBID (Bad Body Image Day)

Anger Is Fire

You had a Bad Body Image Day. You're mad at yourself, disappointed in this journey, heartbroken because you feel like you're swimming against the tide, enraged that things feel so hard, done with all of it. On BBIDs, the task of accepting your body feels difficult, unfair, impossible. You can't tell if it's you or this harsh world, but you are overwhelmed. On BBIDs you feel like the world isn't going to change—so you should.

Welcome to being a totally normal human being! Before acting, take a pause.

Yes, you have every right to feel pissed.
Yes, the world is harsh and unfair.

No, that doesn't mean you failed or you suck.
No, this doesn't mean you should stop doing something that matters to you.

Learn to see the hard days as a sign from your body that you need to dedicate time, energy, and resources to taking care of yourself. That's it.

When the BBIDs come, lean in. Feel your feelings fully. Scream in your car or into a pillow. Put on a sad movie and just cry. Hard moments, hard days, sometimes even hard *years* are normal parts of being a person. You didn't do anything wrong. Learning to let yourself have all kinds of feelings is such an important part of loving and accepting your body. Your body creates feelings as a way to give you information: Mostly it tells you if your needs and wants are being met—or if they're not.

Happiness, contentment, and joy are usually signs your needs are being met.

Anger, sadness, and frustration are usually signs they aren't. Simple.

It's very, very common for *anger* to come up when we're working on our relationship with our bodies. So let's focus on this important, often maligned emotion.

Why does anger come up so often? Anger is the most natural response ever to something messed-up happening. You weren't born feeling like your body didn't measure up. You were *taught* that. You learned absurd, unrealistic, and damaging body ideals from family, peers, school, books, the internet, movies, and TV. That was wrong—nay, it was super messed up! Yet so many of us feel shame when anger arises. Well, let's work on changing that!

Allowing yourself to feel anger is an extraordinary act of self-care and self-acceptance.

You don't need to have *feelings* about your feelings. No need to feel shame on top of feeling angry. Being angry is enough work. You can just let yourself have the emotion, check in about what needs are or aren't being met, and then figure out ways you can get what you need without engaging in self-destructive behavior.

Most of us have been taught that anger is unattractive or maybe just plain unacceptable. What if anger were just information—data—that helped us understand our needs better? Well, it is, actually.

But it's a whole heck of a lot more than that.

Anger is fire. When you feel anger, imagine it as the sun: a bright, burning ball of energy shedding precious light on the not-so-great nooks and crannies of our lives. Fire is an active element—an element that pushes us into action.

This section is about reframing anger as an important emotion that is galvanizing you to change the things in your life that aren't working. Next time you get angry, don't feel fear or shame. Think of the sun—powerful, unrepentant, glowing, and the universal signal that it's time to rise and shine.

Congratulations, You Are Pissed!

Anger is a sign that you're a human with a body that houses complex feelings. A cause for celebration! When did you learn anger was a negative emotion? Do you like thinking of anger more as a positive power source or a neutral data point? Think of a recent time you felt angry. Remember that anger means there's an obstacle between you and your goal. What was the obstacle? What was the goal? Write about what you might have done differently if you saw anger as positive or neutral.

This Journal Is Body Positive

Shame and Anger Are Kissing Cousins

As we let go of body shame, it's normal for that energy to flip directions—from anger directed inward (toward yourself, most often experienced as shame) to anger directed outward. This can feel scary. Just remember that it's OK to be scared, and it's normal to feel a little overwhelmed as this transition happens. This prompt is about redirecting blame away from your body. Who are the real culprits? Instead of being angry at yourself all the time, name the problematic media, cultural norms, or experiences that create that sense of shame.

Example

I feel shame and blame my body for not fitting into the clothes I want, but actually I'm angry that the fashion industry doesn't make clothing in a better variety of sizes.

I feel shame and blame my body for _____

_____

_____

_____

_____

but actually I'm angry that _____

_____

_____

_____

I feel shame and blame my body for _____

_____

_____

_____

_____

but actually I'm angry that _____

_____

_____

_____

I feel shame and blame my body for _____

_____

_____

_____

_____ ,

but actually I'm angry that _____

_____

_____

_____ .

I feel shame and blame my body for _____

_____

_____

_____

_____ ,

but actually I'm angry that _____

_____

_____

_____ .

I feel shame and blame my body for _____

_____

_____

_____

_____,

but actually I'm angry that _____

_____

_____

_____.

I feel shame and blame my body for _____

_____

_____

_____

_____,

but actually I'm angry that _____

_____

_____

_____.

This Law Is Important

Similar to the economic theory known as the law of diminishing returns, there's a point where your investment starts yielding progressively smaller rewards—where you're giving away more than you're getting. Applied to your relationship with your body, this means the longer and harder you try to "fix" your body, the smaller the returns you'll get for this investment over time. How much time and energy do you dedicate to attempting to "fix" your body? Are you getting more than you're giving away? Does it feel worth it? Why or why not? How will you know that you've hit your point of diminishing returns? If you're already there, what might help you move away from the "fix it" mentality?

Don't Weight. Do It Now.

Are there things you imagine doing later, when you have your "dream body"? Wear a certain outfit? Go to a certain place? Do something important to you? What if, instead of waiting, you did those things now, in this body? It's time to change the narrative so you can get more of what you want, sooner. Write out your "dream body" goals. Next to each one, write down whether changing the narrative looks like doing A, B, C, or D. Write down thoughts and any actionable steps you can take to move from dreaming to doing.

A. I can actually do this right now with my current body.

B. I can actually do this right now if I adjust the goal or dream a little bit.

C. I can't do this right now, and I can find a new goal or dream that is meaningful to me.

D. I've thought about it, and this goal or dream just doesn't seem possible to me. I need time to process the loss before I can move forward and create a new goal or dream.

Dream Body Goals

A, B, C, D

Self-Advocacy 101

Self-advocacy is the skill of using your voice to get your needs met. Self-advocacy comes in handy when you encounter a situation where someone's expectations or words don't align with the kind of relationship you have (or want to have) with your body. But it can be hard to do in the moment, especially if you're caught unprepared. We can anticipate some of those situations and prepare beforehand, so we're not left feeling like a deer in headlights. On the following pages, write down some scripts for moments you encounter that are weird, awkward, or hostile.

The first script is your boilerplate. Write down what you want to say when you hear something that doesn't align with the relationship you want to have with your body. Your script could be as simple as, "I don't like that language. Please don't talk about that around me anymore," or "I'm trying something new, where I don't comment on my or other people's bodies. It's been really amazing, and it's something I plan to keep doing," or "I learned recently that I can help support people with body shame or eating disorders by not talking about weight or eating habits."

Then, for each subsequent script, choose a venue or person (e.g., date, school, work; the doctor, your friend, your spouse, a family member, etc.); a belief or phrase you hear often when you're in that place or with that person; and a tone that feels right for how you relate to that arena or person (humorous, sober, professional, academic, vulnerable, guns-blazing). Then write down a few things you'd like to say next time you need to self-advocate. Try to write scripts that feel realistic and that are in your own voice.

→ My boilerplate self-advocacy script:

→ Venue/person 1 _____

When I'm here/with this person, I often hear this: _____
_____

Here's the tone I want to use for self-advocacy: _____
_____

Here's my self-advocacy script: _____
_____
_____
_____

→ Venue/person 2 _____

When I'm here/with this person, I often hear this: _____
_____

Here's the tone I want to use for self-advocacy: _____
_____

Here's my self-advocacy script: _____
_____
_____
_____

→ Venue/person 3

When I'm here/with this person, I often hear this:

Here's the tone I want to use for self-advocacy:

Here's my self-advocacy script:

→ Venue/person 4

When I'm here/with this person, I often hear this:

Here's the tone I want to use for self-advocacy:

Here's my self-advocacy script:

DIY Care Package (to Open on BBIDs)

Bad Body Image Days (BBIDs) are simply that: a twenty-four-hour period when you're feeling particularly tender. Sometimes you'll experience multiple BBIDs in a row. You can stop thinking of these days with dread and recognize that they're a regular part of having a body in a culture that is constantly judging our bodies, and that BBIDs are invitations to practice (our favorite!) self-care. Think of BBIDs as a sick day. What do you do when you have a cold? Stay in bed? Watch movies? Drink tea and soup? What always makes you smile? What always resets you emotionally? What do you do when you want to feel pampered? Start brainstorming what you want in your DIY care package here. List practices, phrases, books, treats, favorite pillows, craft ideas, etc.

Fill Up This Kit with What You Need

The Mixtape

Make a BBID mixtape. Choose the tracks you need: high-powered self-love anthems, tear jerkers, rage against the patriarchy tunes, songs that help you have fun in your body, or whatever else you want to be part of the soundtrack for your BBIDs. Write the song titles on the following cassette tapes. Use this as a guide for making a playlist you can listen to.

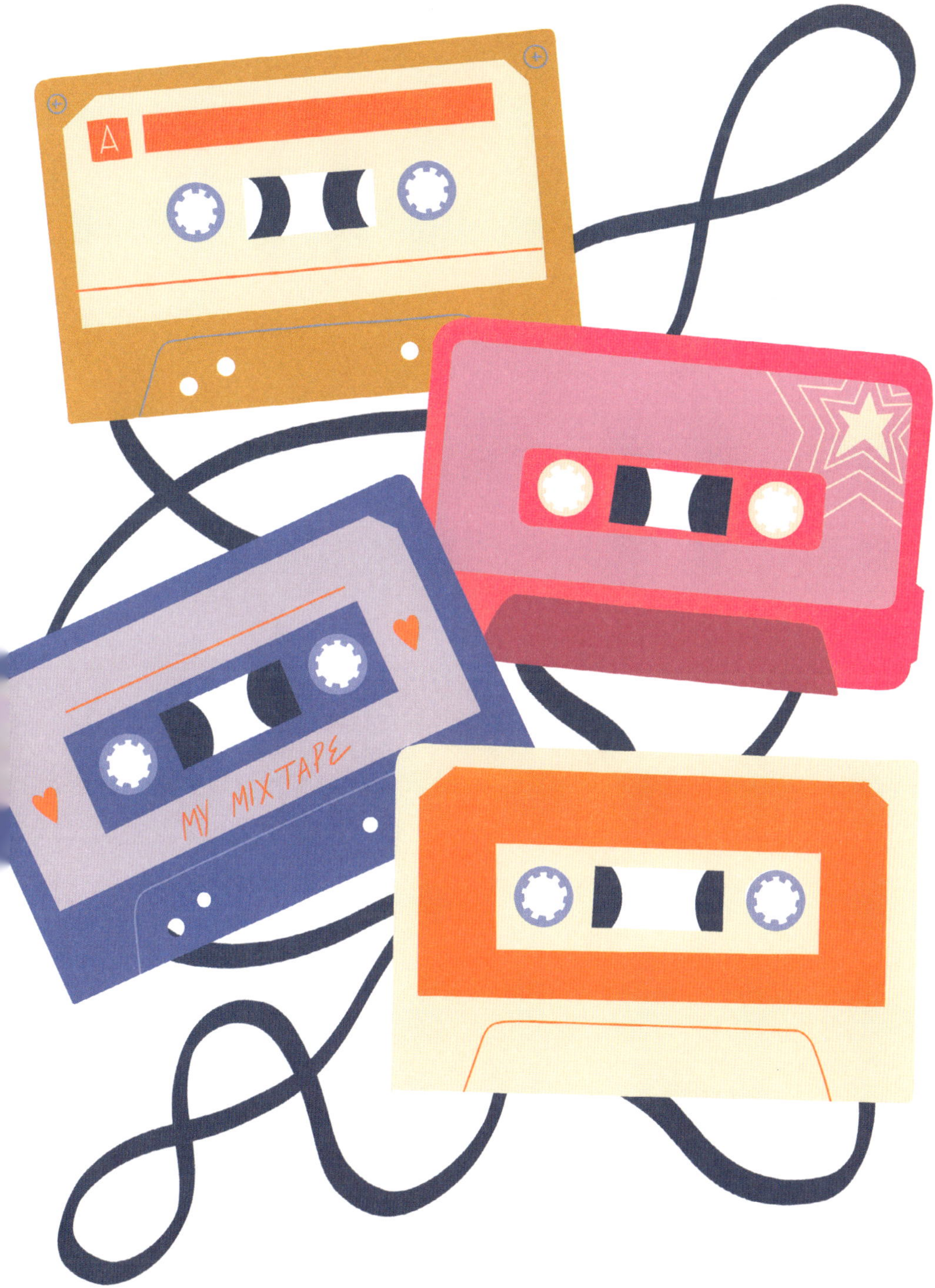
A
MY MIXTAPE

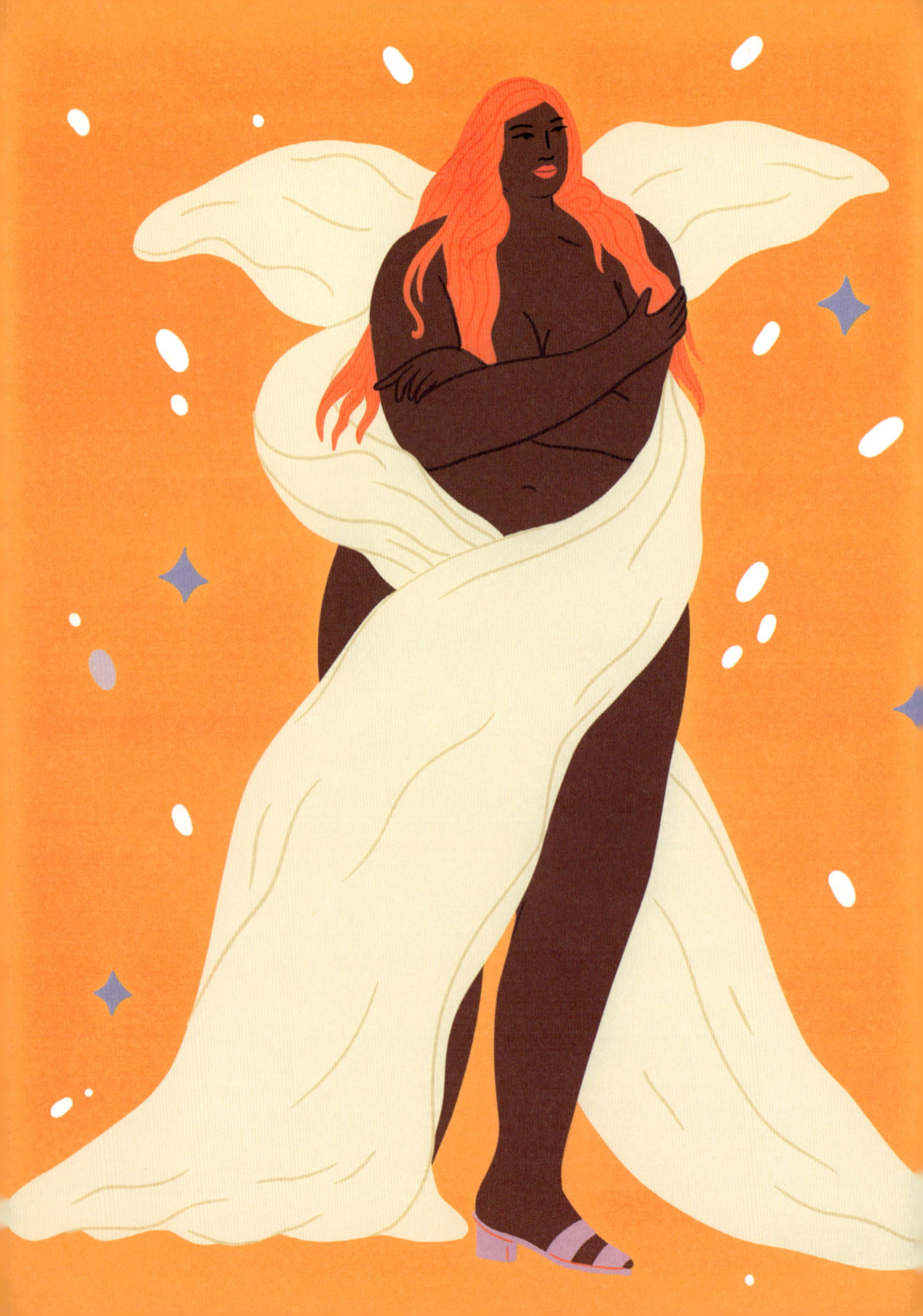

Part 5

Your Body Does Not Exist for Other People. It Exists for You. Protect It.

The High Art of Boundaries

When it comes to your body, *boundaries* is the most powerful B-word out there. To set a boundary is to say to yourself and to others: "My body is precious enough to deserve protection."

Boundaries are about taking care of ourselves: not giving away more than we want and not letting in more than we want. Think of boundaries as an invisible blanket that you wrap around your body, mind, and spirit. A blanket keeps in warmth and privacy—vital things for any person. We can let others under the blanket if we want. Sometimes we're cool with someone just putting their feet—and feet only!—in there with us. Rarely—if a person feels very safe to us—we're down to invite their whole self in there with us. Most often, though, we want the blanket between us and someone else's body, ideas, and feelings.

Whether you realize it or not, you already have boundaries. Let's talk about what that looks like. Before you say yes or no to something or someone, your body creates a sensation. That sensation is a signal, a vital piece of information: "I like this. This feels good"; or, "I don't like this. It doesn't feel good." Whether you act on the signal or not, the signal is there. The body never stops inviting you to listen. Each of us has different boundaries based on how we grew up, what we've been through, and our individual personalities. Your limits are unique and just-right. Though we often feel pressure to push past our limits, it's important to know that your boundaries matter and that boundaries always, *always* make complete sense within the context of your life.

There are different kinds of boundaries. *Physical* and *emotional* are two really important types. Physical boundaries are about who gets to touch you, and when, and how. Emotional boundaries are about thoughts and feelings: who and what is allowed in the vulnerable parts of your heart and your mind.

Use the prompts that follow to help you learn more about your existing boundaries and what you want them to be in the future.

This section is about reflecting on your boundaries: why you have them, why they matter, and what they are.

Who Are Your VIPs?

We live in a world where complete strangers have opinions about you and your body. That might never change, but you don't have to let them penetrate the inner depths of your soul! VIPs are the (very important) people in your inner circle, people who have earned your trust and respect. Unless someone is a VIP, you have every right to ignore their opinion. Write down the qualities you're seeking in future VIPs here. Use the activity on the following pages to home in on your current VIPs.

Qualities for Future VIPs

VIPs

I'm leaning in because these people have earned my trust.

Me

**Acquaintances
Friends
Coworkers**

I'm sort of listening sometimes because some of these people may have some good ideas.

**People I Don't Know
or Barely Know**

I'm not letting any of these people near my mind or spirit.

What Fills Up Your Cup?

It's important to know who and what nourishes you, energizes you, and makes you feel good. Who and what recharges your battery or fills up your cup? List the people, places, things, and activities that do just that.

Who Gets Your Coupons?

Coupons are amazing, but a store can't give every single person who walks through their doors an unlimited supply of coupons or it would go bankrupt. Similarly, learning to have a good relationship with your body means limiting the emotional resources you're giving to others. Think of your coupon as a kind of an emotional freebie, a Get Out of Jail Free card, that you give to others. It grants another person *one* radical act of compassion, forgiveness, grace, or understanding when they have done something that doesn't feel good to you. You get to decide how many coupons you have and how many you want to give out. For instance, you could have a rule that says, "A new friend gets three coupons. I will be gracious and overlook things that bother me on three occasions during the beginning of our friendship. If they earn my trust, I will probably give them more coupons." You get to decide the terms or fine print of the coupon. For instance, you could have a rule that says, "I don't limit the number of coupons I give to my partner," or "I usually like to give people this many coupons, but if someone goes too far, I might cut off their coupons completely." Start noticing where your coupons are going—and begin to limit how many you give away. Decorate the following coupons however you want. Make them memorable! Next time you give someone a coupon, think of this page.

Nº 283

This coupon entitles the bearer to _____ radical act(s) of understanding

COUPON OF

COUPON OF

FREE

Know Thyself

Part of existing for yourself and not for others is understanding that you are a unique person. There has never been another person who has your exact body, traits, and thoughts, and there never will be ever again. So your job now is to name the unique combination of qualities that make you . . . you. Create a unique shape as you connect the dots, and feel free to add traits and qualities that are important to you.

homebody

optimist

hopeless
romantic
                                    plant parent
                                                                resilient

        serious
                        extrovert
                                                            fur baby
                                                            parent
pessimist
                    masc
                            introvert
        nature lover
                                                        tender
                scaredy-cat
Team
Trauma
                                                    giggly

        adventurous
                        ocean lover
small
                                                weird
                babe
        in-between
                            morning
                            person   sweet lover

                salt lover
fan of coffee
                                night owl
                                                    nonbinary

            queer
teetotaler   straight
                        big

        world traveler   bookworm
                    femme

The Awkward Art of Redirection and Not Engaging

Many people live in sheer terror of that moment when someone makes a body-shaming comment and expects you to respond and go along with it. Like, the moment when someone tees up a body-shaming call-and-response ("Have you lost weight?" or "I feel so fat!"), expecting you to swing and hit the ball back. This moment is 100% going to come up! Your job is to practice engaging with these moments in a way that feels good to you, with the knowledge that no one in history has ever died of feeling awkward. So, here's the assignment: Write down your worst fears about what will happen if you just don't engage the next time this kind of social exchange happens. Next to those fears, write down a pep talk (for you) and some ideas for redirection (for them).

Fear

Pep Talk

Ideas for Redirecting the Conversation

Fear

Pep Talk

Ideas for Redirecting the Conversation

Fear

Pep Talk

Ideas for Redirecting the Conversation

Fear

Pep Talk

Ideas for Redirecting the Conversation

Fear

Pep Talk

Ideas for Redirecting the Conversation

Fear

Pep Talk

Ideas for Redirecting the Conversation

Fear

Pep Talk

Ideas for Redirecting the Conversation

You 100% Got This

Creating a good relationship with your body goes against every single cultural rule and norm. Congratulations! You're doing something deeply rewarding, disruptive, amazing, cool, and—uh-huh, you guessed it—challenging. The good news is: You've got this. Reflect back on what you've learned and highlight at least one experience that has equipped you for this journey.

You've Got This, Babe!

Illustration by Lucila Perini

Virgie Tovar is an author, an activist, and the founder of Babecamp, a self-guided online course designed to help people break up with diet culture. Her books include *Hot & Heavy: Fierce Fat Girls on Life, Love & Fashion*; *You Have the Right to Remain Fat*; and *The Self-Love Revolution: Radical Body Positivity for Girls of Color*. She created and hosts the podcast *Rebel Eaters Club*. She lives in San Francisco. For more of her work, check out her website and follow her on Instagram:

www.virgietovar.com
@virgietovar

POPCORN

you are FIRE